This B-baLL booK
BeLONGS to

Dedicated to lovers of the game,
who appreciate it in all its forms
—C. R. S. Jr.

HOOP

QueeNS

Poems by
Charles R.
Smith Jr.

CANDLEWICK PRESS
CAMBRIDGE, MASSACHUSETTS

CONTENTS

Margo
Dydek

FLY Swatter

Looming
large in lane,
trying to contain
fly balls floating
into domain,
Fly Swatter
swats
away everything
guarding the house
with one mighty swing.
Standing seven foot two inches
from toe to head
SMACK
SLAP
SWAT!
kills points dead.

Rejecting finger-rolls
on the rise,
paint penetrations
get **pulverized,**
lay-up attempts
brought down to size
while keeping opponents
from two-point prize,
wingspan swings
high in sky,
swatting away
annoying flies,
batting them down
knocking them down
slamming shots high
in the air
to the ground,

throwing them out
sending them back
flicking off flies
on the attack,
Fly Swatter stings
with one mighty
THWACK
sending a message:
DON'T
COME
BACK!!

9

BOUNCE TO THIS

Braids bounce on break
as ball bounces from shake
and b-bake moves
fueled by **Philly-Funkdafied grooves,**
changing no-look passes
into easy twos.
Handle honed
from paying dues
on hardwood dance floors
in Italy
Brazil
Spain
and France,
rhythmic feet d-dance
circles around opponents
in basketball sh-shoes
moving to the beat of
St-Staley's Groove,
on and on
and **on and on**
bouncing with rhythm
'til the **break of Dawn.**

Dawn
Staley

Graceful gazelle
gallops and glides
fast past defenders
with effortless strides.
Sly and swift
and standing tall,
eyes on alert,
nose sniffing for ball.
Positioned in paint
ready to score,
on misses and bricks
bouncing from boards.
Two points scored
on rebound and putback,
using animal instincts
while attacking the rack.

ON
THE
ATTACK

Lisa
Leslie

THE CHEF

Racing and running
and spinning and swerving
in total control
while feeding and serving
delicious assists
with wrist-flick tricks,
Chef T serves
dishes with slick

**Ticha
Penicheiro**

style and
skill,
finesse and
flair,
feeding teammates
while twisting midair.
Slicing
and **dicing**
and **shaking**
and **flipping,**
mixing
and **tossing**
and **chopping**
and **whipping**
no-look passes
underhand passes
teaching skip-stop
behind-the-back classes,
serving sweet treats
putting points on the board,
keeping hungry teammates
coming back for more.

ALL that

Sheryl Swoopes

Ladies and Gentlemen

and other spectators,
feast your eyes on Sheryl,
the Trey Maker
Dribble Drive Creator,
up Fake
take-it-to-the-hole
penetrator.

through-the-lane
coming-right-at-ya.
The Lane Spinner
championship Winner,
coast to coast
off-the-glass
finger-roll finisher.
The Ball Stripper
Defense Slipper,
right-side fadeaway

The Point Leader
Stat Line Feeder,
last-second
shot-making
OT Buzzer-Beater.
The Board Snatcher
Bullet Pass Catcher,
charging hard

net-cord-ripper.
The Shot Blocker
De-fensive Stopper,
ball hawk
swooping-downcourt
stop-and-popper . . .
Swoopes to the Hoop
the MVP Jaw-Dropper.

17

Yolanda Griffith

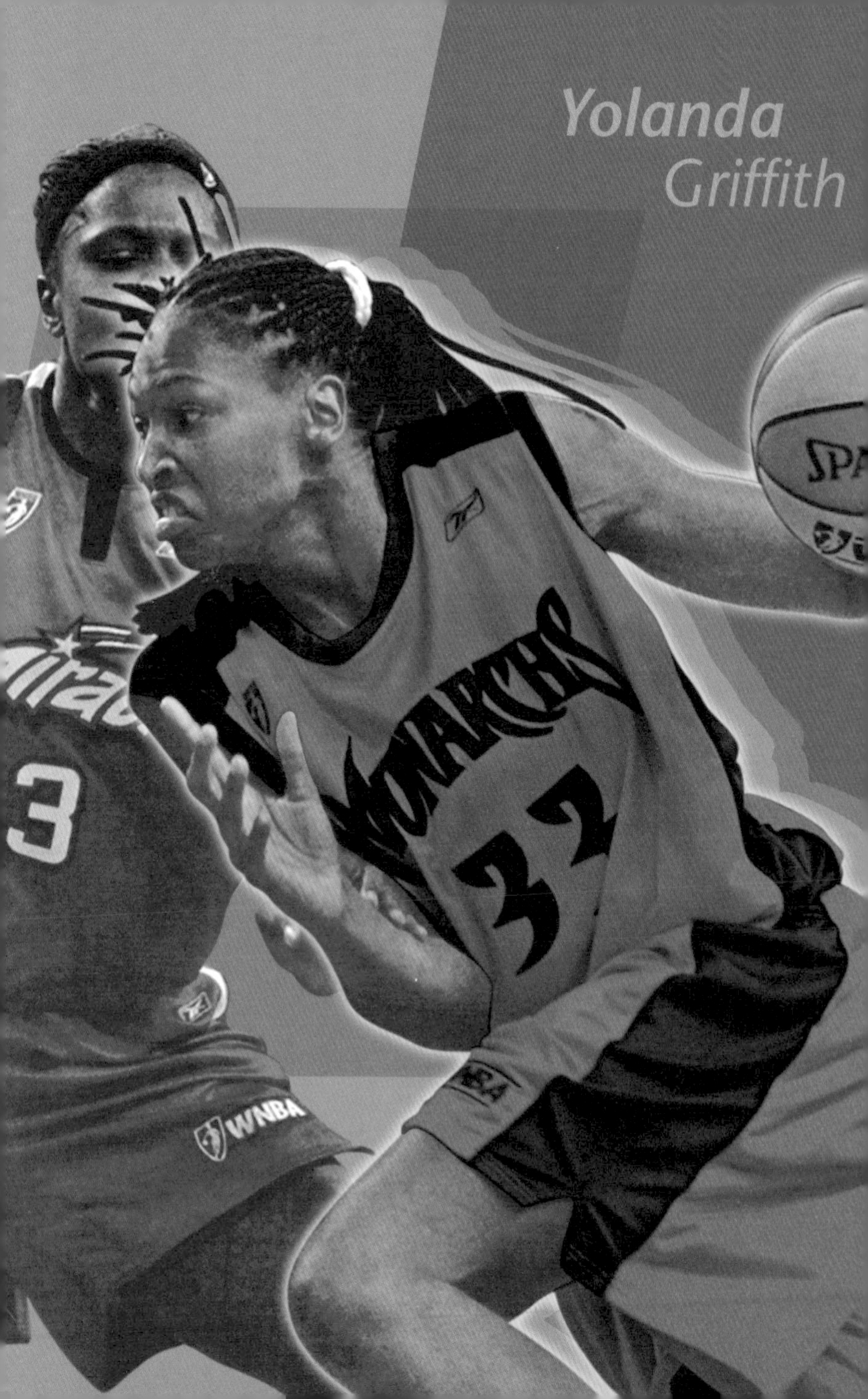

Standing tall at six foot four
double-threat trouble steps onto the floor.
Long limbs stretch with elastic agility,
racking up points with athletic ability.
Ripping down rebounds with strength and skill,
putting back points with power at will.
Six foot four and standing tall,
flashing finesse and power with the ball.

DOUBLE
TROUBLE

Board-bouncing catches
strike acrobatic matches
when Chamique sparks flame
into white-hot game;
a wildfire spreading
that can't be contained.
Racing
reversing
leaping
and snaking,
jumping
twirling
taking
and making
long-distance fireballs
ignited with spin,
burning nylon
from baseline
again
and again.

Finger-roll finish
for last-second win,
rising and floating
like smoke
to the rim.
Blazing a trail
with moves that scorch,
another hot performance
from The Human Torch.

FIRE

STARTER

Tina
Thompson

T for 2
2 points for T,
jumper gets drained
from top of the key.
T for 2
2 points for T,
toes behind line
make it a 3.

T for 2
2 points for T,
loss for you
win for T.

Strong gusts of wind
begin
when
cornrow-shaped clouds
spin
and form
as T-Spoon
steps on court
to perform,
swirling
and **stirring**
into a storm,
striking
with lightning-quick hands
that **swarm**
and **swipe**
at ball
with intensity,
blowing over opponents
with torturous D.

Swooping
on ball
with a thunderous roa
blasting downcourt
looking to score.
Rushing and **busting**
through
like a hurricane,
twisting and **turning**
midair
in the lane,
rising and **rising**
up high
to the rim,
leaving a trail
of destruction again.

Teresa
Weatherspoon

Nykesha
Sales

Eyes spy prize
with laserlike precision
focused on rim
for impossible mission,
down by **2**,
4 *seconds on the clock,*
weaving through traffic,
trying to lock
in on target,
zero in on goal,
3 *seconds left*
to put ball
into hole,

2 *seconds left,*
no time to think,
target locked
ready to shoot
missile loaded
BLINK BLINK
1 *second*
left on clock
feet stop
toes spot
up behind the line,
knees bent
shoulders square
missile launched at twine.
Shot's up.
Shot's in
from hands cool and calm,
another **1***-point victory*
from Long-Distance Bomb.

The
BOMB

Skitter-skatter soles
dart
through defensive holes
bounce-bouncing ball
with silky smooth soul,
bounce-bouncing ball
between legs
behind back
with stutter-step moves
to make ankles snap.
Ball rock-rocking
right-left-right
soles stand still
then **BLAST**

out of sight,
blowing past barriers
of flat-footed defenders,
fleet feet

ATTACK

until they surrender
to constant chaotic
charges to the cup,
Nik-Nik
on the quick-quick
in control
from the soles up.

SOLE
CONTROLLER

Nikki
McCray

WORKING

Lunch pail toting
hardhat wearing
fierce
rebounding machine,
punches clock
to chase the rock
and wipe the windows
clean.
Leaping
and lunging
around the blocks
until the job is done,
doing damage underneath
until the war is won.
Working hard
to get the ball
and motivate
the team,
**overpowering
glass scouring**
boards
until they gleam.

Game over,
final total
of rebounds
at nineteen,
just another
day at work
for the window washing
Plexi polishing
board demolishing
queen.

Natalie
Williams

30

Poem Notes

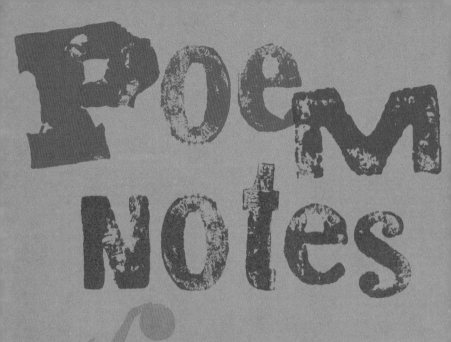

Margo Dydek *Fly Swatter* The idea for Margo Dydek's poem came from her being so tall. When she stands beneath the basket with her arms in the air, she can be quite intimidating. Shot blockers reject shots by swatting them away, so I imagined the balls that were coming toward the basket as flies and therefore she became the Fly Swatter.

Yolanda Griffith *Double Trouble* Yolanda Griffith is a new breed of player who can cause damage in a number of ways. In her case, she has the agility to score points from anywhere on the floor, and she also has the power to grab rebounds. That spells Double Trouble for the competition.

Chamique Holdsclaw **Fire Starter** I've seen Chamique Holdsclaw play since she was in college, and what has stuck out most is how fast she puts points on the board. In a short time, she can "catch fire" and score several baskets. Since she can score from anywhere on the floor, this makes it easy to rack up the points quickly and easily, so whenever she gets going, she turns into a "fire starter."

Lisa Leslie **On the Attack** The first thing that comes to mind when I think of Lisa Leslie is how graceful and elegant she looks. But make no mistake, when she steps on the court, she plays like an animal. She reminds me of a gazelle because they are very swift and move with ease, just like her.

Nikki McCray **Sole Controller** I had a lot of fun doing the research for Nikki McCray's poem because she plays as though she's still on the playground. The way she dribbles the ball and the energy she plays with make her exciting to watch. Several of the moves that I've seen her do were created off the dribble, and when she scored the points, the defense had to adjust. That means that whatever her feet do has an effect on the game.

Ticha Penicheiro **The Chef** Ticha Penicheiro's poem was easy to write because she has a very flashy game. But instead of taking shots, she sets her teammates up for them. I call her the chef because she uses a variety of skills to move the ball around and "feed" her teammates. I followed this image all the way through the poem by drawing on the techniques a chef would use to create a meal.

Nykesha Sales **The Bomb** *Having a great jump shot is like having a weapon; you have an advantage over your opponent. Nykesha Sales has a great jump shot and has used it on several occasions to win the game at the buzzer. Just as fighter planes' missile launchers are equipped with locking devices enabling them to track their targets, once Nykesha Sales locks onto HER target, the hoop, she won't miss.*

Dawn Staley **Bounce to This** *I remember the first time I saw Dawn Staley play and the way she handled the ball. She bounced the ball with a unique rhythm that separated her from others. Since she is from Philadelphia, I used that, and since she has played in different countries, I used that as well. Several players use musical rhythms to help them on the court, so I referred to the court as a dance floor where everyone is doing their own thing.*

Sheryl Swoopes **All That** *The term "all that" describes Sheryl Swoopes to a T. She does so many things so well that I just listed them in a creative way and described her game as "all that." From ball handling to rebounding to shooting the ball, she does all these jobs well and with a style all her own.*

Tina Thompson **T 4 2** *When I first started watching Tina Thompson play, I noticed the announcer would say "T for 2" whenever she scored a two-pointer. So the use of letters and numbers and the rhythm of the song "Tea for Two" led to Tina Thompson's poem.*

Teresa Weatherspoon **Hurricane T** *Hurricanes have lots of power and energy, and anyone who has seen "T-Spoon" play knows that this describes her perfectly. Not only is she fast on the court, but she also plays with such emotion that she is like a storm brewing beneath the surface, ready to explode at any moment.*

Natalie Williams **Working Overtime** *When it comes to getting rebounds, height, strength, and jumping ability don't matter nearly as much as simply WANTING the ball. Since rebounding is such tough work, I imagined Natalie Williams as a blue-collar worker putting in her time at a construction site, just going about her business, working hard.*

CHARLES R. SMITH JR.

Growing up in California, I spent many hours
reading anything I could get my hands on.
Reading books filled with stories and poems
inspired me to write my own. The more I read,
the more I wrote. If I wasn't reading a book,
I was playing a sport. I played everything,
particularly basketball, and spent many
afternoons on the court, perfecting my
jump shot. While working on my
high school yearbook staff as a writer,
I was introduced to photography and
immediately decided to make a career
out of it. After graduating from photography school, I headed to New York to
pursue my dream of being a professional
photographer. I continued with my writing
and, with a heavy influence from rap music,
began writing poetry instead of stories.
Now I have combined my photographic
skills with my love of reading, writing, and
sports to create an exciting career.

Text copyright © 2003 by Charles R. Smith Jr.
www.charlesrsmithjr.com

Photograph of Margo Dydek copyright © 2003 by AP/Wide World Photos/Paul Warner
Photograph of Dawn Staley copyright © 2003 by AP/Wide World Photos/Nell Redmond
Photograph of Lisa Leslie copyright © 2003 by AP/Wide World Photos/Ric Francis
Photographs of Ticha Penicheiro, Yolanda Griffith, and Natalie Williams copyright
© 2003 by AP/Wide World Photos/Steve Yeater
Photograph of Sheryl Swoopes copyright © 2003 by AP/Wide World Photos/Chuck Burton
Photograph of Chamique Holdsclaw copyright © 2003 by AP/Wide World Photos/
Rick Bowmer
Photograph of Tina Thompson copyright © 2003 by AP/Wide World Photos/
Greg Wahl-Stephens
Photograph of Teresa Weatherspoon copyright © 2003 by AP/Wide World Photos/
John Greilick
Photograph of Nykesha Sales copyright © 2003 by AP/Wide World Photos/Susan Walsh
Photograph of Nikki McCray copyright © 2003 by AP/Wide World Photos/John Harrell

First paperback edition 2007

The Library of Congress has cataloged the hardcover edition as follows:

Library of Congress Catalog Card Number 2002041111

ISBN 978-0-7636-1422-5 (hardcover)

ISBN 978-0-7636-3561-9 (paperback)

10 9 8 7 6 5 4 3 2 1

Printed in China

This book was typeset in Stone Sans.

Digital artwork and typography by Caroline Lawrence

Candlewick Press, 2067 Massachusetts Avenue, Cambridge, Massachusetts 02140

visit us at www.candlewick.com